THE FANTASTICALLY FUNNY JOKE BOOK

Over 750 Gigglesome Gags!

ARCTURUS

ARCTURUS

This edition published in 2023 by Arcturus Publishing Limited
26/27 Bickels Yard, 151–153 Bermondsey Street,
London SE1 3HA

Written by Lisa Regan
Designed by Trudi Webb
Edited by Rebecca Clunes and Violet Peto
Illustrations from Shutterstock

ISBN: 978-1-3988-2744-8
CH011254NT
Supplier 29, Date 1122, PI 00002931

Printed in China

CONTENTS

WHAT DO YOU GET IF YOU CROSS T-REX AND AN EVIL WITCH?

I DON'T KNOW, BUT I'D DEFINITELY RUN AWAY FROM IT!

DIVE IN HEADFIRST TO FIND HUNDREDS MORE LAUGHS LIKE THIS. THE SIX SENSATIONAL, SNIGGER-TASTIC SECTIONS ARE PACKED FULL OF CHUCKLES AND GROANS TO SHARE WITH YOUR LOVED ONES, OR TO KEEP YOU GIGGLING TO YOURSELF AT NIGHT.

SO, NEXT TIME YOUR FRIENDS ALL MOAN THAT THERE'S NO WI-FI, KEEP THEM ENTERTAINED WITH THE MOST HEE-LARIOUS JOKES ON THE PLANET. IT'S TRUE!

CHAPTER 1

IN THE KITCHEN

WAITER, DO YOU SERVE LOBSTERS HERE?

YES, SIR, WE SERVE ANYBODY.

WAITER, WHAT'S THIS?

IT'S BEAN SOUP, SIR.

I DON'T CARE WHAT IT'S BEEN! WHAT IS IT NOW?

WAITER, I CAN'T EAT THIS FOOD. PLEASE CALL THE MANAGER.

IT'S NO USE, HE CAN'T EAT IT EITHER.

WAITER, THERE'S A SNAIL IN MY SALAD!

THAT'S OK, IT WON'T EAT MUCH.

WAITER, IS THERE PIZZA ON THE MENU?

NO, I WIPED IT OFF.

WAITER, WILL MY PIZZA BE LONG?

NO, IT WILL BE ROUND.

WAITER, THIS BREAD IS STALE!

IT WASN'T LAST WEEK.

WAITER, THIS FOOD TASTES FUNNY.

THEN WHY AREN'T YOU LAUGHING?

WHAT DID THE CANNIBAL ORDER AT THE RESTAURANT?

PIZZA WITH EVERYONE ON IT.

DID YOU HEAR ABOUT THE HILARIOUS BANANA?

IT HAD THE WHOLE FRUIT BOWL IN PEELS OF LAUGHTER!

HOW DO YOU MAKE A WALNUT LAUGH?

CRACK IT UP!

WHAT DO YOU GET IF YOU CROSS A SNAKE AND AN APPLE TART?

A PIE-THON!

WHICH DAY OF THE WEEK DO EGGS HATE?

FRY-DAY!

BUT WHY SHOULDN'T YOU TELL JOKES TO EGGS?

BECAUSE THEY MIGHT CRACK UP!

HOW DO YOU MAKE AN EGG LAUGH?

TELL IT A YOLK!

DID YOU HEAR ABOUT THE EGG THAT LOVED TO PLAY TRICKS?

IT WAS A PRACTICAL YOLKER!

WHICH PEOPLE LIKE TO EAT SNAILS?

THE ONES THAT DON'T LIKE FAST FOOD!

WHAT DO CHIMPS WEAR WHEN THEY'RE COOKING?

APE-RONS!

WHAT DID THE NUT SAY WHEN IT HAD A COLD?

"CASHEW!"

WHY DID THE BANANA HAVE TO GO TO THE HOSPITAL?

BECAUSE IT WASN'T PEELING WELL!

WHAT DO YOU CALL CHEESE THAT BELONGS TO SOMEONE ELSE?

NACHO CHEESE! (NOT YOUR CHEESE—GEDDIT?!)

WHY DID THE GRAPE TRY NOT TO SNORE?

IT DIDN'T WANT TO WAKE UP THE REST OF THE BUNCH!

WHY DID THE GIRL LOVE HOT CHOCOLATE?

BECAUSE SHE WAS A COCOA-NUT!

WHY DID MOTHER GRAPE GO ON A SPA RETREAT?

SHE WAS TIRED OF RAISIN KIDS!

WHAT DO SNOWMEN EAT FOR BREAKFAST?
FROSTED FLAKES!

WHAT DO YOU GET IF YOU MIX BIRDSEED WITH CEREAL?
SHREDDED TWEET!

WHAT FAST FOOD DO SNOWMEN PREFER?
ICE-BURGERS!

WHAT DID ONE SNOWMAN SAY TO THE OTHER?
"CAN YOU SMELL CARROT?"

WAITER, THERE'S A DEAD FLY IN MY SOUP!

SORRY, ARE YOU A VEGETARIAN?

WAITER, THERE'S A TWIG IN MY MEAL!

JUST A MOMENT, I'LL GET THE BRANCH MANAGER.

WAITER, THERE'S AN ANT IN MY SOUP!

I KNOW ... THE FLIES STAY AWAY DURING THE WINTER.

WAITER, WHY IS THERE FISH ON MY PLATE OF LASAGNE?

I'M SORRY, SIR, IT DOESN'T KNOW IT'S PLAICE.

19

WHAT DO DOGS EAT AT THE MOVIES? PUPCORN!

A CHEESEBURGER WALKS INTO A BAR AND ASKS FOR ORANGE JUICE.

THE BARTENDER SAYS, ""I'M SORRY, WE DON'T SERVE FOOD HERE."

WHY DID THE TURKEY JOIN A BAND?

HE HAD HIS OWN DRUMSTICKS!

WHY DID THE GIRL STARE AT THE CARTON OF JUICE?

BECAUSE IT SAID CONCENTRATE.

HOW DO YOU FIX A BROKEN PIZZA?

WITH TOMATO PASTE!

WHAT DID THE VINAIGRETTE SAY TO THE REFRIGERATOR?

"CLOSE THE DOOR, I'M DRESSING!"

WHAT CAN YOU SERVE BUT NEVER EAT?

A TENNIS BALL.

WHAT DO YOU CALL A REALLY LARGE PUMPKIN?

A PLUMPKIN!

WHERE DO TOMATOES HANG OUT ON SUNDAY?

THE SALAD BAR!

WHAT KIND OF ICE CREAM DO BIRDS LIKE THE MOST?

CHOCOLATE CHIRRUP!

DID YOU HEAR ABOUT THE CANNIBAL WEDDING?

THEY TOASTED THE BRIDE AND GROOM!

WHAT'S RED AND DANGEROUS?

SHARK-INFESTED TOMATO SOUP!

WHY DIDN'T THE CHEF PUT HERBS IN THE FOOD?

HE DIDN'T HAVE THE THYME!

WHAT DID THE MARTIAL ARTS TEACHER BUY FROM THE BUTCHER?

KARATE CHOPS!

WHERE DO BABY COWS GO FOR LUNCH?

THE CALF-ETERIA!

WHY DID THE CUCUMBER CRY?

BECAUSE IT WAS IN A PICKLE!

HOW DO YOU KNOW THAT AN ELEPHANT HAS RAIDED YOUR REFRIGERATOR?

THERE ARE FOOTPRINTS IN THE CHEESECAKE.

HOW DO YOU EVEN FIT AN ELEPHANT IN THE REFRIGERATOR?

OPEN THE DOOR, AND PUSH IT REALLY HARD!

HOW DO YOU FIT A GIRAFFE IN THE REFRIGERATOR?

TAKE THE ELEPHANT OUT FIRST!

WHAT DID THE BEE SAY WHEN IT ARRIVED BACK AT THE HIVE?

HI HONEY, I'M HOME!

WHY COULDN'T THE TEDDY BEAR FINISH ITS LUNCH? BECAUSE IT WAS STUFFED!

WHAT KIND OF CHEESE DO YOU USE TO LURE A BEAR AWAY? CAMEMBERT! ("COME ON BEAR!")

WHY DID THE WALNUT GO OUT WITH A RAISIN? IT COULDN'T FIND A DATE!

WHAT'S THE DIFFERENCE BETWEEN AN ELEPHANT AND A GRAPE? A GRAPE SQUASHES IF YOU SIT ON IT!

WAITER, THERE'S A FLY IN MY SOUP!

YES, SIR. IT LOOKS LIKE IT COMMITTED INSECTICIDE.

WAITER, I THINK I JUST SWALLOWED A FISH BONE!

ARE YOU CHOKING?

NO, I'M SERIOUS!

WAITER, MY BOWL IS WET!

I BEG YOUR PARDON, MISS. THAT'S THE SOUP.

WAITER, THERE'S A FLY IN THIS BUTTER.

YES, I BELIEVE IT'S A BUTTERFLY.

WHAT DID THE SPIDER ORDER AT THE FAST FOOD RESTAURANT?

A BURGER AND FLIES!

SHAKESPEARE WALKED INTO A DINER AND ASKED FOR A DRINK.

THE MAN BEHIND THE COUNTER SHOOK HIS HEAD. "YOU'RE BARD!"

WHY DID THE BOY GIVE MUSTARD TO HIS DOG WHEN IT HAD A FEVER?

IT WAS A HOT DOG!

WHAT DID THE EGG SAY TO THE WHISK?

"I KNOW WHEN I'M BEATEN!"

WHAT SWEET TREAT DO DOGS FIND DELICIOUS?

PUP-CAKES!

WHY DID THE BAKER STOP MAKING DONUTS?

HE WAS TIRED OF THE HOLE BUSINESS!

WHY DID THE BAKER GET FIRED FROM HER JOB?

SHE WAS A LOAFER!

HOW DO YOU KNOW IF A CANNIBAL FEELS LIKE EATING YOU?

HE BUTTERS YOU UP!

WHY DID THE SAUSAGE ROLL?

BECAUSE IT SAW THE MILKSHAKE!

ARE CARROTS REALLY GOOD FOR YOUR EYESIGHT?

WELL, HAVE YOU EVER SEEN A RABBIT WEARING GLASSES?

WHERE DID THE SPAGHETTI GO TO DANCE?

TO A MEATBALL!

WHAT DID THE CAVEMAN CHOOSE FROM THE MENU?

A CLUB SANDWICH!

WHY DO DINOSAURS EAT RAW MEAT?

THEY DON'T KNOW HOW TO COOK!

WHAT CAN A WHOLE APPLE DO THAT HALF AN APPLE CAN'T DO?

IT CAN LOOK ROUND.

WHICH SALAD IS THE BEST AT PLAYING POOL?

THE CUE-CUMBER!

WHAT DO FIREFIGHTERS EAT WITH THEIR CHEESE?

FIRECRACKERS!

CHAPTER 2

GET WELL SOON

DOCTOR, THE INVISIBLE MAN IS HERE FOR HIS APPOINTMENT.

TELL HIM I CAN'T SEE HIM RIGHT NOW.

WHY DID THE CLOWN CALL EMERGENCY SERVICES? HE BROKE HIS FUNNY BONE!

DOCTOR, I HAVE NO ENERGY. I CAN'T EVEN WALK DOWN THE ROAD WITHOUT GETTING TIRED.

IT'S BECAUSE YOU'RE WEARING LOAFERS!

DOCTOR, IT HURTS WHEN I GO TO THE BATHROOM.

URINE TROUBLE.

WHY DID THE VAN BOUNCE DOWN THE ROAD? IT WAS A HICCUP TRUCK!

WHAT DID THE DOCTOR PACK FOR HER TRIP TO THE DESERT?

A THIRST-AID KIT!

DID YOU HEAR ABOUT THE MAN THAT WAS HIT ON THE HEAD BY AN ICICLE?

IT KNOCKED HIM OUT COLD!

DOCTOR, THERE'S A MAN WHO URGENTLY NEEDS YOU TO TREAT SCRATCHES ALL OVER HIS BODY.

WHAT'S HIS NAME?

CLAUDE!

WHAT DID THE DOCTOR SAY TO THE VOLCANO?

"YOU NEED TO QUIT SMOKING!"

DID YOU HEAR ABOUT THE MAN WHO SWALLOWED URANIUM?

HE GOT ATOMIC ACHE!

WHAT'S RED AND THICK?

A BLOOD CLOT!

IF CHICKENPOX ARE FILLED WITH CLEAR FLUID, WHAT ARE CATPOX FILLED WITH?

PUS!

WHAT BLOOD GROUP DO INSECTS HAVE?

AB!

WHEN DOES A DOCTOR GET ANGRY?

WHEN SHE RUNS OUT OF PATIENTS!

WHY ARE THE TONSILS EXCITED?

THEY'VE HEARD THE DOCTOR IS TAKING THEM OUT ON FRIDAY!

DOCTOR, I KEEP HEARING A RINGING SOUND!

THEN ANSWER YOUR PHONE, DUMMY.

DID YOU HEAR THE JOKE ABOUT THE GERMS?

DON'T WORRY, I DON'T WANT YOU TO SPREAD IT AROUND!

WHAT NOISE DID THE TRAIN MAKE WHEN IT HAD A COLD?

AAAA-CHOO-CHOO!

WHY DID THE TRAIN WORKER GET AN ELECTRIC SHOCK?

HE WAS THE CONDUCTOR!

IF AN ATHLETE SUFFERS FROM ATHLETE'S FOOT, WHAT DOES A SOLDIER SUFFER FROM?

MISSILE-TOE!

WHY DID THE HANDYMAN SEE A PSYCHIATRIST?

HE HAD A SCREW LOOSE!

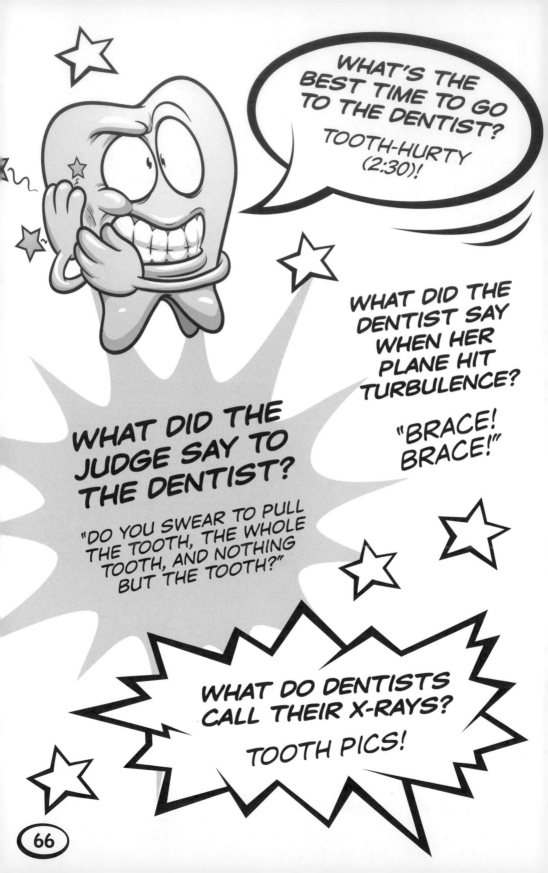

WHY DID THE ROCKET VISIT THE DOCTOR?

TO GET ITS BOOSTER SHOT!

WHY WAS THE DOCTOR WORRIED ABOUT THE OBESE ALIEN?

IT WAS AN EXTRA-CHOLESTEROL!

WHAT DID THE ALIEN SAY WHEN IT NEEDED BLOOD TESTS?

"TAKE ME TO YOUR BLEEDER!"

HOW DO YOU TREAT AN ALIEN WITH CLAUSTROPHOBIA?

GIVE IT SOME SPACE!

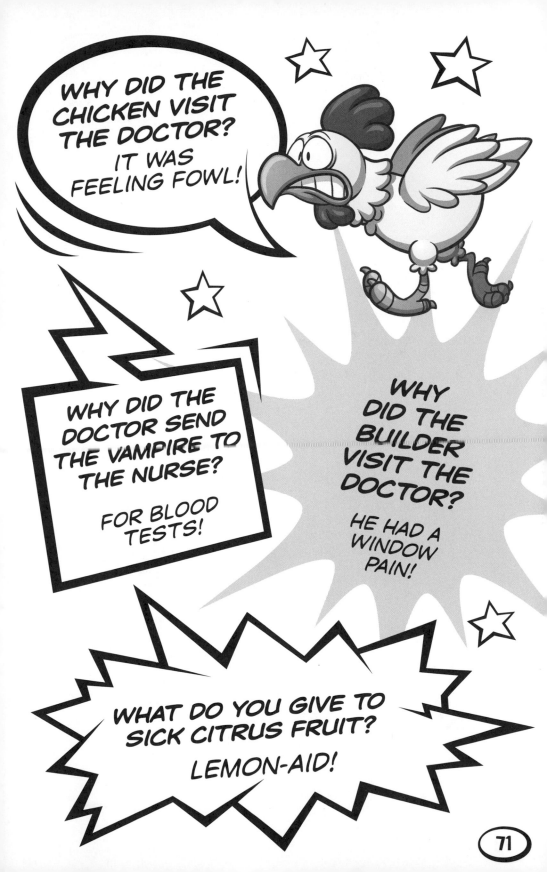

WHY DID THE PONY VISIT THE DOCTOR?

IT WAS A LITTLE HOARSE!

WHAT DID THE DOCTOR PRESCRIBE FOR THE PONY?

COUGH STIRRUP!

THE PONY'S COUGH GOT WORSE. WHAT HAPPENED NEXT?

IT WAS TAKEN TO THE HORSE-PITAL!

HORSE: DOCTOR, I SLEEP ALL DAY AND I'M AWAKE ALL NIGHT.

DOCTOR: YOU'RE A NIGHTMARE!

73

75

WHAT DID THE SAILOR SAY AS HE THREW UP ON A WINDY DAY?
"IT'S ALL COMING BACK TO ME NOW!"

WHAT DO YOU GET IF YOU CROSS A COMEDIAN AND GERMS?

A SICK JOKE!

WHAT'S LOUD AND STICKY AND FULL OF GERMS?

A COUGH DROP!

WHICH IS FASTER, HOT OR COLD?

HOT, BECAUSE ANYONE CAN CATCH A COLD!

WHAT DID THE DOCTOR SAY WAS WRONG WITH THE CAR MECHANIC?

HE'D HAD A BREAKDOWN!

THE MECHANIC ASKED FOR A SECOND OPINION.

"HMM," SAID THE DOCTOR. "YOU'RE OVERTIRED."

THE CAR MECHANIC TOLD HIS WIFE WHAT THE DOCTOR SAID.

"YES," SHE AGREED. "YOU DO SEEM EXHAUSTED."

DOCTOR, I KEEP THINKING I'M A BRIDGE!

WHAT'S COME OVER YOU? A LARGE BUS AND SIX CARS!

WHEN SHOULD YOU GO TO SEE A BIRD DOCTOR?

WHEN YOU'RE A PUFFIN!

WHAT DO ELEPHANTS TAKE TO HELP THEM SLEEP?

TRUNKQUILIZERS!

WHY DID THE MUMMY THINK IT HAD A COLD?

BECAUSE OF ITS COFFIN!

DID YOU HEAR ABOUT THE BEAR THAT ENDED UP IN A HOSPITAL?

IT HAD A GRIZZLY ACCIDENT!

WHAT'S GREEN AND HAS FOUR LEGS AND A TRUNK?
A SEASICK ELEPHANT!

EXCUSE ME, WHAT'S THE QUICKEST WAY TO THE HOSPITAL?
LIE DOWN ON THAT BUSY ROAD OVER THERE.

WHAT DO YOU CALL A MAN WHO HAS LEFT THE HOSPITAL?
MANUEL!

WHAT DO YOU CALL A SICK CROCODILE?
AN ILLIGATOR!

DOCTOR, I DREAMED I WAS A PEANUT BUTTER SANDWICH.

I THINK YOU MIGHT BE GOING NUTS!

DOCTOR, MY SNORING IS SO BAD, I'M KEEPING MYSELF AWAKE!

I THINK YOU'D BETTER SLEEP IN ANOTHER ROOM!

DOCTOR, I'M REALLY AFRAID THAT I'VE TURNED INTO A VAMPIRE.

NECKS PLEASE!

DOCTOR, I THINK MY EYESIGHT IS GETTING WORSE.

IT CERTAINLY IS, THIS IS A POLICE STATION!

WHY DID THE NURSE TIPTOE PAST THE MEDICINE CABINET?

HE DIDN'T WANT TO WAKE THE SLEEPING PILLS!

WHAT'S THE MEDICAL NAME FOR A FEAR OF SANTA CLAUS?

CLAUS-TROPHOBIA.

DOCTOR, FIRST MY SISTER WAS OBSESSED WITH TANGLED, NOW SHE'S TOTALLY INTO FROZEN.

HOW LONG HAS SHE SUFFERED FROM THESE DISNEY SPELLS?

IF YOU DON'T FEEL WELL, WHAT DO YOU PROBABLY HAVE?

A PAIR OF GLOVES ON YOUR HANDS!

WHY DID THE GERM CROSS THE MICROSCOPE?

TO GET TO THE OTHER SLIDE!

WHAT DO YOU CALL A GERM THAT LOVES 1960S FASHION?

A RETROVIRUS!

WHAT DID THE BOAT'S CAPTAIN DO WHEN HE WAS SICK?

HE WENT IN TO SEE THE DOCK!

WHAT TV SHOWS DO GERMS HATE?

SOAP OPERAS!

WHAT'S WORSE THAN A HIPPO WITH A COLD?

A GIRAFFE WITH A SORE THROAT!

WHAT HAPPENS WHEN MUSIC TEACHERS ARE SICK?

THEY SEND IN A NOTE!

DID YOU HEAR ABOUT THE GARDENER WHO HAD A COLD?

HE CAUGHT IT FROM THE GERMANIUMS!

WHAT SHOULD YOU DO IF A HIPPO SNEEZES?

GET OUT OF THE WAY!

CHAPTER 3

ON THE FARM

WHAT DID THE MEXICAN FARMER SAY TO HIS CHICKEN?

"OH, LAY!"

WHAT DID THE SHEEP FARMER SAY WHEN SOMEONE LEFT THE GATE OPEN?

"EWE HAVE RUINED MY DAY!"

HOW DOES A FARMER TALK TO HIS ANIMALS?

HE USES AN INTER-PET-ER.

FARMER HARRY: HOW MUCH STRAW DID YOU MAKE YESTERDAY?

FARMER FRANK: STACKS!

HOW DO CHICKS SAVE MONEY ON THEIR SHOPPING?

THEY USE COOP-ONS!

WHY DID THE GUM CROSS THE ROAD?

IT WAS STUCK TO THE CHICKEN'S FOOT!

DID YOU HEAR ABOUT THE HEN THAT FELL INTO A CEMENT MIXER?

IT BECAME A BRICK LAYER!

WHY WOULDN'T THE HEN CROSS THE ROAD?

BECAUSE IT WAS CHICKEN!

HOW DO FLEAS GET FROM ONE DOG TO ANOTHER?

THEY ITCH HIKE!

HOW DOES THE FARM DOG GET INTO THE HOUSE?

THROUGH THE LABRA-DOOR!

WHAT HAPPENED TO THE SHEEPDOG THAT RAIDED THE CANTALOUPE FIELD?

IT FELT MELON-COLLIE.

WHAT KIND OF DOG MAKES YOU SAY "OUCH!"?

A DOBERMAN PINCHER!

98

WHAT DID THE VET SAY TO THE GOAT FARMER?
"HOW ARE THE KIDS?"

HOW DO YOU MAKE ANTIFREEZE?
LOCK HER IN THE BARN OVERNIGHT.

HOW DOES A PERUVIAN FARMER WAKE UP IN THE MORNING?
WITH A LLAMA-CLOCK!

FARMER: HOW DO YOU HIRE AN EXTRA WORKER?
FARMER'S SON: SEND HIM UP A LADDER?

DID YOU HEAR ABOUT THE CAT WITH EIGHT LEGS?

IT WAS AN OCTO-PUSS.

WHAT DOES A CAT HAVE IN ITS BED?

A CATTER-PILLOW.

WHAT DID THE FARMER CALL HIS CAT THAT ATE GRASS?

A LAWN MEOWER!

WHAT DID THE CAT SAY WHEN THE FARMER STOOD ON ITS PAW?

"MEE-OW!"

WHICH SPORT DO HORSES PLAY?
STABLE TENNIS!

DID YOU HEAR ABOUT THE PONY THAT RAN AROUND THE WORLD?
IT WAS A GLOBETROTTER!

WHAT DID THE FARMER SAY WHEN HIS HORSE LAY DOWN?
"GIDDY-UP!"

HOW LONG SHOULD A HORSE'S LEGS BE?
LONG ENOUGH TO REACH THE GROUND!

WHAT DID THE GRUB SAY WHEN ITS FRIEND GOT STUCK IN AN APPLE?

"WORM YOUR WAY OUT OF THAT ONE!"

HOW DO DAIRY FARMERS HELP EACH OTHER?

THEY COW-OPERATE!

WHAT HAS 3 HEADS, 2 ARMS, 2 TAILS, AND 8 LEGS?

A FARMER ON HIS HORSE WITH A CHICKEN UNDER HIS ARM!

WHAT DID THE CLEAN DOG SAY TO THE DIRTY DOG?

"LONG TIME, NO FLEA!"

WHERE DOES A SHEEP FARMER HAVE HIS HAIR CUT?

AT THE BAA-BAAS!

HOW DO SHEEP STAY WARM IN WINTER?

CENTRAL BLEATING!

WHERE DO SHEEP GO FOR A BREAK?

THE BAA-HAA-MAAS!

WHY DID THE FARMER TAKE HIS SHEEP INDOORS DURING THE STORM?

HE DIDN'T WANT ANY WET BLANKETS!

WHY DID THE CAT SPEND CHRISTMAS AT THE BEACH? HE WANTED TO SEE SANDY CLAWS!

DID YOU HEAR ABOUT THE WELL-BEHAVED CAT? IT WAS PURR-FECT.

DID YOU HEAR ABOUT THE CAT THAT DRANK THREE SAUCERS OF WATER REALLY QUICKLY?

IT SET A NEW LAP RECORD!

WHAT DO YOU GET IF YOU GIVE LEMON JUICE TO A CAT?

A SOURPUSS!

WHY DID THE DOG SIT IN THE SHADE?

IT DIDN'T WANT TO BE A HOT DOG!

WHY DON'T DOGS TRAVEL BY PLANE?

BECAUSE THEY GET JET WAG!

WHY DID THE DOG JUMP IN THE POND?

IT SAW A CATFISH!

WHAT DO YOU CALL A SHEEPDOG IN A COUNTRY MEADOW?

A COLLIE-FLOWER!

DID YOU HEAR ABOUT THE BEEKEEPER WITH STICKY HAIR?

HE USED A HONEY COMB!

WHAT DO YOU CALL A BEE AND A HORSE THAT LIVE NEAR EACH OTHER?

NEIGH BUZZ!

WHAT DID THE BEES DO WHEN THEY MOVED TO A NEW HIVE?

THEY HAD A HOUSE-SWARMING PARTY!

DID YOU HEAR ABOUT THE BEE THAT MOANED INSTEAD OF BUZZED?

IT WAS A GRUMBLEBEE!

HOW DO YOU GET OVER AN ELECTRIC FENCE?

VOLT!

WHAT DID THE SHEEP FARMER DO WHEN THE SUN SHONE?

HE HAD A BAA-BECUE!

WHAT HAS EARS BUT CAN'T HEAR A THING?

A CORNFIELD!

DID YOU HEAR ABOUT THE STAMPEDE AT THE DAIRY FARM?

IT WAS UDDER CHAOS!

WHY DO RABBITS HAVE FUR COATS?

BECAUSE THEY'D LOOK RIDICULOUS IN LEATHER JACKETS!

WHAT DO YOU CALL A RABBIT IN A BAKERY?

A STICKY BUNNY!

DID YOU HEAR ABOUT THE RABBIT THAT STOLE THE FARMER'S CARROTS AND THEN RAN AWAY?

IT ESCAPED TO THE HAREPORT!

WHY DID THE TWO RABBITS VISIT A NEW FARM?

THEY WERE ON THEIR BUNNYMOON!

121

WHAT DO YOU CALL A CATTLE THIEF?

A BEEF BURGLAR!

WHAT DO COWS PLAY AT PARTIES?

MOO-SICAL CHAIRS!

WHAT GOES "OOO, OOO"?

A COW WITH NO LIPS!

WHY DID THE CATTLE FARMER LAUGH AT HIS HERD?

HE FOUND THEM VERY A-MOO-SING!

WHAT DO SCARECROWS LIKE TO EAT?

STRAW-BERRIES!

WHY DID THE SCARECROW WANT TO STAND IN A CORNFIELD?

BECAUSE IT WAS A-MAIZE-ING!

WHY DID THE SCARECROW WIN A PRIZE?

BECAUSE HE WAS OUTSTANDING IN HIS FIELD!

WHY DON'T SCARECROWS NEED FEEDING?

BECAUSE THEY'RE ALREADY STUFFED!

WHY COULDN'T THE FARMER'S DAUGHTER REACH THE BEEF FROM THE TOP SHELF?

THE STEAKS WERE TOO HIGH!

WHERE DO YOU PAY FOR BABY HENS?

AT THE CHICK-OUT!

WHY DID THE FARMER KEEP SHEEP IN THE HENHOUSE?

TO GET ROOST LAMB!

HOW DOES A FARMER SING IN TUNE?

HE USES A PITCHFORK!

CHAPTER 4

AT SCHOOL

HOW DO YOU GET STRAIGHT A'S?

USE A RULER!

WHY DIDN'T THE NOSE WANT TO GO TO SCHOOL?

IT GOT PICKED ON!

HOW DO TREES GET ON THE INTERNET?

THEY LOG IN!

WHAT COUNTRY DO PIRATES STUDY IN GEOGRAPHY?

ARRRRGENTINA!

WHAT SUBJECT DO PIRATES LIKE BEST?

ARRRRRT!

WHY DID THE TEACHER JUMP INTO THE POOL?
HE WANTED TO TEST THE WATER!

WHAT IS A POLYGON?
A DEAD PARROT.

TEACHER: WHAT LANGUAGE DO THEY SPEAK IN CUBA?

STUDENT: CUBIC!

WHY WAS THE STUDENT LIKE A SEAHORSE?
HIS GRADES WERE ALL BELOW C-LEVEL.

135

TEACHER: HAVE YOU PUT CLEAN WATER IN THE FISH TANK?

STEVE: NO, IT HASN'T DRUNK THE FIRST TANKFUL YET.

WHY DID THE BOY EAT HIS HOMEWORK?

HIS TEACHER SAID IT WAS A PIECE OF CAKE!

TEACHER: DIDN'T I TELL YOU TO STAND AT THE END OF THE QUEUE?

JAMIE: I TRIED, BUT THERE WAS SOMEBODY THERE ALREADY!

WHICH COUNTRY DO GEOGRAPHY TEACHERS LIKE BEST?

EXPLA-NATION!

WHAT HAPPENED WHEN THE BABY WENT TO SCHOOL? THERE WAS A CRY-SIS!

WHAT KIND OF TEACHER ENJOYS REGISTRATION? ONE THAT IS ABSENT-MINDED!

TEACHER: WHICH WAS THE FIRST ANIMAL IN SPACE? EMMA: THE COW THAT JUMPED OVER THE MOON?

WHAT'S BLACK AND WHITE AND HARD? A PHYSICS TEST!

WHY DID THE ASTRONAUT WALK OUT OF CLASS?

IT WAS LAUNCH TIME!

WHY WAS IT SO EASY FOR SHERLOCK HOLMES TO LEARN HIS ALPHABET?

BECAUSE IT WAS L-M-N-TRY.

WHAT DO PIXIES LEARN AT SCHOOL?

THE ELF-ABET!

WHY DO PIRATES STRUGGLE TO LEARN THEIR ALPHABET?

BECAUSE THEY GET STUCK AT C!

WHY DID THE CLOCK GET SENT OUT OF THE CLASSROOM?

BECAUSE IT WAS TOCKING TOO MUCH!

IF SLEEP IS REALLY GOOD FOR THE BRAIN, WHY WON'T THEY ALLOW IT IN CLASS?

WHAT DOES THE VEGETARIAN TEACHER SAY AT SUNDAY SCHOOL?

"LETTUCE PRAY!"

TEACHER: WHY DID YOU JUST EAT YOUR PENCIL SHARPENER?

JASON: I WAS TRYING TO SHARPEN MY APPETITE BEFORE LUNCH!

TEACHER: WHAT WAS THE ROMANS' GREATEST ACHIEVEMENT?

JORDAN: LEARNING TO SPEAK LATIN!

WHICH ROMAN EMPEROR SUFFERED FROM HAY FEVER?

JULIUS SNEEZER!

TEACHER: WHEN DID CAESAR REIGN?

ALICIA: I DIDN'T KNOW HE RAINED, I THOUGHT IT WAS HAIL, CAESAR!

WHO REFEREED THE TENNIS MATCH BETWEEN CALIGULA AND NERO?

THE ROMAN UMPIRE!

WHICH TOILET PAPER DO MATHEMATICS TEACHERS PREFER?

MULTI-PLY!

WHY DID THE GEOMETRY TEACHER STAY AT HOME?

SHE HAD SPRAINED HER ANGLE!

WHY DID THE SCIENCE TEACHER WEAR SUNGLASSES?

BECAUSE HIS CLASS WAS SO BRIGHT!

TEACHER: IF I HAD 6 APPLES IN ONE HAND AND 8 APPLES IN THE OTHER, WHAT WOULD I HAVE?

SALLY: ENORMOUS HANDS, SIR!

WHAT WAS CARVED ON A KNIGHT'S GRAVE IF HE DIED IN BATTLE?

RUST IN PEACE!

WHY WERE THE EARLY DAYS OF HISTORY CALLED THE DARK AGES?

BECAUSE THERE WERE SO MANY KNIGHTS!

WHICH OF KING ARTHUR'S KNIGHTS INVENTED THE ROUND TABLE?

SIR CUMFERENCE!

WHY DID THE COOK FEED THE DRAGON HOT SALSA?

HE WANTED TO BARBEQUE SOME CHICKEN.

TEACHER: ANYONE WHO HASN'T DONE THEIR HOMEWORK WILL BE IN BIG TROUBLE.

JOE: HOW CAN WE GET IN TROUBLE FOR SOMETHING WE DIDN'T DO?

WHY DID THE TEACHER WRITE ON THE WINDOW?

BECAUSE SHE WANTED HER LESSON TO BE CLEAR.

WHY DO ALL CLASSROOMS HAVE BRIGHT LIGHTS?

BECAUSE THE PUPILS ARE SO DIM!

WHY WAS THE SKELETON KEPT BACK A YEAR?

BECAUSE IT WAS A NUMBSKULL!

HOW WAS THE ROMAN EMPIRE DIVIDED UP?

WITH A PAIR OF CAESARS!

WHAT HAPPENED WHEN THE WHEEL WAS INVENTED?

IT CAUSED A REVOLUTION!

HOW DID THE VIKINGS COMMUNICATE?

BY NORSE CODE!

TEACHER: HOW LONG DID THE PHILOSOPHER ARISTOTLE LIVE?

MEGAN: ALL HIS LIFE!

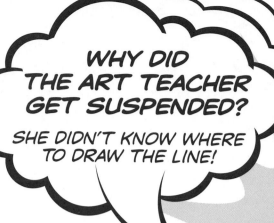

WHY DID THE ART TEACHER GET SUSPENDED?

SHE DIDN'T KNOW WHERE TO DRAW THE LINE!

ART TEACHER: HOW WOULD YOU DRAW A BELCH?

ROSIE: WITH A BURPLE PEN!

HOW DO YOU IMPRESS AN ART TEACHER?

EASEL-Y!

WHERE DO ART TEACHERS GO FOR A BREAK?

COLORADO!

155

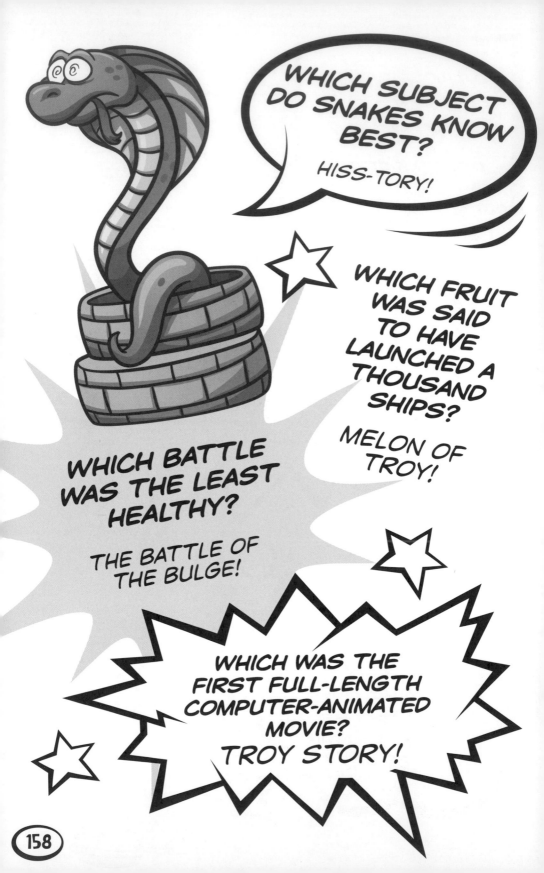

WHY DID CHARLIE WALK BACKWARD ON HIS WAY TO SCHOOL?

IT WAS BACK TO SCHOOL DAY!

WHERE IS THE EASIEST PLACE TO FIND DIAMONDS?

IN A DECK OF CARDS!

WHY DID THE GIRL STUDY IN HER BEDROOM INSTEAD OF THE LIVING ROOM?

SHE WANTED A HIGHER EDUCATION!

TEACHER: WHY DOES YOUR HOMEWORK LOOK LIKE YOUR DAD WROTE IT?

KATHY: I USED HIS PEN, SIR!

WHAT DID THE MOTHER HURRICANE SAY TO HER SON? "I'VE GOT MY EYE ON YOU!"

GEOGRAPHY TEACHER: HOW DO YOU CUT THE OCEAN IN HALF?

SALLY: WITH A SEA SAW, SIR!

WHAT KIND OF HAIR DOES A MARINE BIOLOGIST HAVE?

WAVY!

WHAT DID THE BOY SAY WHEN HE SAW SOME RAINDROPS ON THE WINDOW?

"TWO'S COMPANY, THREE'S A CLOUD!"

SORRY I'M LATE, TEACHER, I OVERSLEPT.

WHAT, YOU MEAN YOU SLEEP AT HOME AS WELL?

OUR TEACHER TALKS TO HERSELF.

SO DOES OURS, BUT SHE THINKS WE'RE LISTENING!

DAD: HOW DID YOUR EXAMS GO?

HARVEY: I ALMOST GOT IN THE TOP 10 IN EVERY SUBJECT! WELL—I GOT ZERO EACH TIME.

TEACHER: I'D LIKE TO GO THROUGH A WHOLE LESSON WITHOUT TELLING YOU OFF.

SAM: BE MY GUEST.

WHAT DO YOU GET WHEN YOU DIVIDE THE CIRCUMFERENCE OF A JACK-O'-LANTERN BY ITS DIAMETER?

PUMPKIN PI!

WHAT'S THE DEFINITION OF ASYMMETRY?

A PLACE WHERE YOU BURY DEAD MATHEMATICS TEACHERS!

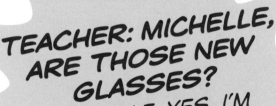

TEACHER: MICHELLE, ARE THOSE NEW GLASSES?

MICHELLE: YES, I'M HOPING THEY'LL IMPROVE DI-VISION!

TEACHER: SEVEN IS AN ODD NUMBER, BUT HOW DO YOU MAKE IT EVEN?

STACEY: TAKE AWAY THE "S"!

WHAT SUBJECT DO ATHLETES LIKE THE BEST?

JOG-RAPHY!

TEACHER: WHY DIDN'T YOU STOP THE BALL?

GOALIE: I THOUGHT THAT'S WHAT THE NET IS FOR?

TEACHER: WHICH POSITION DO YOU PLAY?

BOB: I'VE BEEN TOLD I'M THE MAIN DRAWBACK, SIR.

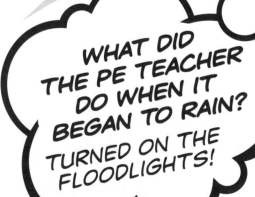

WHAT DID THE PE TEACHER DO WHEN IT BEGAN TO RAIN?

TURNED ON THE FLOODLIGHTS!

BEN: I DON'T THINK I DESERVED A ZERO.

TEACHER: I AGREE, BUT IT WAS THE LOWEST MARK I COULD GIVE YOU!

WHO INVENTED FRACTIONS?
KING HENRY THE FIFTH!

WHY IS BRITAIN SO WET?
BECAUSE THE QUEEN HAS REIGNED THERE FOR SO LONG!

WHERE DID MEDIEVAL KNIGHTS PARK THEIR CAMELS?
CAMELOT!

CHAPTER 5

KNOCK, KNOCK!

KNOCK, KNOCK.
WHO'S THERE?
DONALETTE
DONALETTE WHO?
DONALETTE THE BED
BUGS BITE!

KNOCK, KNOCK.
WHO'S THERE?
ANYA.
ANYA WHO?
ANYA MARKS, GET SET, GO!

KNOCK, KNOCK.
WHO'S THERE?
ALF.
ALF WHO?
ALF FEED YOUR HAMSTER WHILE YOU'RE AWAY!

KNOCK, KNOCK.
WHO'S THERE?
ALISON.
ALISON WHO?
ALISON AT THE DOOR TO HEAR WHEN YOU WERE COMING.

KNOCK, KNOCK.
WHO'S THERE?
ADAM.
ADAM WHO?
ADAMESSY ACCIDENT, CAN I COME IN?

KNOCK, KNOCK.
WHO'S THERE?
BARBARA.
BARBARA WHO?
BARBARA BLACK SHEEP, HAVE YOU ANY WOOL?

KNOCK, KNOCK.
WHO'S THERE?
WENDY.
WENDY WHO?
WENDY WANT ME TO BRING THAT DVD TO YOU?

179

187

KNOCK, KNOCK.
WHO'S THERE?
EAMONN.
EAMONN WHO?
EAMONN MY WAY TO THE STORE. DO YOU WANT ANYTHING?

KNOCK, KNOCK.
WHO'S THERE?
ABA.
ABA WHO?
ABA-D DECISION CAN CAUSE ALL KINDS OF PROBLEMS.

KNOCK, KNOCK.
WHO'S THERE?
MANDY.
MANDY WHO?
MAN, DE TRAFFIC IS AWFUL TONIGHT!

CHAPTER 6

WHO'S THERE?

KNOCK, KNOCK.
WHO'S THERE?
ARCH.
ARCH WHO?
ARE YOU CATCHING
A COLD?

205

KNOCK, KNOCK.
WHO'S THERE?
THEODORE.
THEODORE WHO?
THEODORE IS STUCK. PUSH IT FROM YOUR SIDE!

KNOCK, KNOCK.
WHO'S THERE?
ARIANNA.
ARIANNA WHO?
ARIANNA BUNCH OF HIS FRIENDS ARE GOING TO THE PARK. YOU COMING?

KNOCK, KNOCK.
WHO'S THERE?
LUKE.
LUKE WHO?
LUKE THROUGH THE WINDOW, AND YOU'LL SEE!

225

CHAPTER 7

LOL! KNOCK, KNOCK JOKES

KNOCK, KNOCK.
WHO'S THERE?
AUGUSTA
AUGUSTA WHO?
AUGUSTA WIND BLEW
MY HAT AWAY!

KNOCK, KNOCK.
WHO'S THERE?
BEN.
BEN WHO?
BEN WONDERING WHERE YOU WERE LAST MONTH?

KNOCK, KNOCK.
WHO'S THERE?
TURNER.
TURNER WHO?
TURNER ROUND VERY SLOWLY, THERE'S A ZOMBIE BEHIND YOU!

KNOCK, KNOCK.
WHO'S THERE?
LINDA.
LINDA WHO?
LINDA HAND, I'VE GOT LOADS OF LUGGAGE TO CARRY!

251